POPE FRANCIS
AN

G000124134

POPE FRANCIS
Christmas Homilies and Addresses

VERITAS

Published 2017 by Veritas Publications
7–8 Lower Abbey Street, Dublin 1, Ireland
publications@veritas.ie
www.veritas.ie

ISBN 978 1 84730 820 7

10 9 8 7 6 5 4 3 2 1

A catalogue record for this book is available from the British Library.

Designed by Lir Mac Cárthaigh, Veritas

Printed in Ireland by KC Print, Killarney, Co. Kerry

Veritas books are printed on paper made from the wood pulp of managed forests. For every tree felled, at least one tree is planted, thereby renewing natural resources.

CONTENTS

PART I: CHRISTMAS HOMILIES OF POPE FRANCIS

'Jesus is the Light': 24 Dec 2013 9

'Do I Allow God to Love Me?': 24 Dec 2014 15

'All Sadness Has Been Banished': 24 Dec 2015 21

'A Child Has Been Born to Us': 24 Dec 2016 25

PART II: GENERAL AUDIENCES OF POPE FRANCIS

'We Need Not Be Afraid': 11 Dec 2013 33

'God the Father is Generous': 18 Dec 2013 39

'Jesus was Born in a Family': 17 Dec 2014 45

'He is the Font of Love and Serenity': 30 Dec 2015 51

'Comfort, Comfort My People …': 7 Dec 2016 57

'He Who Brings Peace': 14 Dec 2016 65

'Christ's Birth is the Source of Hope': 21 Dec 2016 73

PART III: 'URBI ET ORBI'
MESSAGES OF POPE FRANCIS FOR 25 DECEMBER

'Peace to Mankind': 25 Dec 2013 81

'Jesus is the Salvation': 25 Dec 2014 89

'Where God is Born, Hope is Born': 25 Dec 2015 95

'Peace to Men and Women': 25 Dec 2016 103

PART I:
Christmas Homilies of Pope Francis

Midnight Mass, Solemnity of
the Nativity of the Lord

'Jesus is the Light'

'The people who walked in darkness have seen a great light.' (Is 9:1)

THIS PROPHECY OF ISAIAH NEVER CEASES TO touch us, especially when we hear it proclaimed in the liturgy of Christmas Night. This is not simply an emotional or sentimental matter. It moves us because it states the deep reality of what we are: a people who walk, and all around us – and within us as well – there is darkness and light. In this night, as the spirit of darkness enfolds the world, there takes place anew the event which always amazes and surprises us: the people who walk see a great light. A light which makes us reflect on this mystery: the mystery of *walking* and *seeing*.

Walking. This verb makes us reflect on the course of history, that long journey which is the history of salvation, starting with Abraham, our father in faith, whom the Lord called one day to set out, to go forth from his country towards the land which he would show him. From that time on, our identity as believers has been that of a people making its pilgrim way towards the promised land. This history has always been accompanied by the Lord! He is ever faithful to his covenant and to his promises. Because he is faithful, 'God is light, and in him there is no darkness at all' (1 Jn 1:5). Yet on the part of the people there are times of both light and darkness, fidelity and infidelity, obedience, and rebellion; times of being a pilgrim people and times of being a people adrift.

In our personal history too, there are both bright and dark moments, lights and shadows. If we love God and our brothers and sisters, we walk in the light; but if our heart is closed, if we are dominated by pride, deceit, self-seeking, then darkness falls within us and around us. 'Whoever hates his brother' – writes the Apostle John – 'is in the darkness; he walks in the darkness, and does not know the way to go, because the darkness has blinded his eyes' (1 Jn 2:11). A people who walk, but as a pilgrim people who do not want to go astray.

On this night, like a burst of brilliant light, there rings out the proclamation of the Apostle: *'God's grace has been revealed, and it has made salvation possible for the whole human race'* (Tit 2:11).

The grace which was revealed in our world is Jesus, born of the Virgin Mary, true man and true God. He has entered our history; he has shared our journey. He came to free us from darkness and to grant us light. In him was revealed the grace, the mercy, and the tender love of the Father: Jesus is Love incarnate. He is not simply a teacher of wisdom, he is not an ideal for which we strive while knowing that we are hopelessly distant from it. He is the meaning of life and history, who has pitched his tent in our midst.

The shepherds were the first to see this 'tent', to receive the news of Jesus' birth. They were the first because they were among the last, the outcast. And they were the first because they were awake, keeping watch in the night, guarding their flocks. The pilgrim is bound by duty to keep watch and the shepherds did just that. Together with them, let us pause before the Child, let us pause in silence. Together with them, let us thank the Lord for having given Jesus to us, and with them let us raise from the depths of our hearts the praises of his fidelity: We bless you, Lord God most high, who lowered yourself for our sake. You are immense, and you made yourself small; you are rich and you made yourself poor; you are all-powerful and you made yourself vulnerable.

On this night let us share *the joy of the Gospel*: God loves us, he so loves us that he gave us his Son to be our brother, to be light in our darkness. To us the Lord repeats: 'Do not be afraid!' (Lk 2:10). As the angels said to the shepherds: 'Do not be afraid!'. And I also repeat to all of you: Do not be afraid! Our Father is patient, he loves us, he gives us Jesus to guide us on the way which leads to the promised land. Jesus is the light who brightens the darkness. He is mercy: our Father always forgives us. He is our peace. Amen.

Vatican Basilica, Tuesday, 24 December 2013

'Do I Allow God to Love Me?'

'THE PEOPLE WHO WALKED IN DARKNESS have seen a great light; those who dwelt in a land of deep darkness, on them has light shined' (Is 9:1). 'An angel of the Lord appeared to [the shepherds] and the glory of the Lord shone around them' (Lk 2:9). This is how the liturgy of this holy Christmas night presents to us the birth of the Saviour: as the light which pierces and dispels the deepest darkness. The presence of the Lord in the midst of his people cancels the sorrow of defeat and the misery of slavery, and ushers in joy and happiness.

We too, in this blessed night, have come to the house of God. We have passed through the darkness which envelops the earth, guided by the flame of faith which illuminates our steps, and enlivened by the hope of finding the 'great light'. By opening our hearts, we also can contemplate the miracle of that child-sun who, arising from on high, illuminates the horizon.

The origin of the darkness which envelops the world is lost in the night of the ages. Let us think back to that dark moment when the first crime of humanity was committed, when the hand of Cain, blinded by envy, killed his brother Abel (cf. Gen 4:8). As a result, the unfolding of the centuries has been marked by violence, wars, hatred and oppression. But God, who placed a sense of expectation within man made in his image and likeness, was waiting. God was waiting. He waited for so long that perhaps at a certain point it seemed he should have given up. But he could not give up because he could not deny himself (cf. 2 Tim 2:13). Therefore he continued to wait patiently in the face of the corruption of man and peoples. The patience of God. How difficult it is to comprehend this: God's patience towards us.

Through the course of history, the light that shatters the darkness reveals to us that God is Father and that his patient fidelity is stronger than darkness and corruption. This is the message of Christmas night. God does not know outbursts of anger or impatience; he is always there, like the father in the parable of the prodigal son, waiting to catch from afar a glimpse of the lost son as he returns; and every day, with patience. The patience of God.

Isaiah's prophecy announces the rising of a great light which breaks through the night. This light is born in Bethlehem and is welcomed by the loving arms of Mary, by the love of Joseph, by the wonder of the shepherds. When the angels announced the birth of the Redeemer to the shepherds, they did so with these words: 'This will be a sign for you: you will find a baby wrapped in swaddling clothes and lying in a manger' (Lk 2:12). The 'sign' is in fact the humility of God, the humility of God taken to the extreme; it is the love with which, that night, he assumed our frailty, our suffering, our anxieties, our desires and our limitations. The message that everyone was expecting, that everyone was searching for in the depths of their souls, was none other than the tenderness of God: God who looks upon us with eyes full of love, who accepts our poverty, God who is in love with our smallness.

On this holy night, while we contemplate the Infant Jesus just born and placed in the manger, we are invited to reflect. How do we welcome the tenderness of God? Do I allow myself to be taken up by God, to be embraced by him, or do I prevent him from drawing close? 'But I am searching for the Lord' – we could respond. Nevertheless, what is most important is not seeking him, but rather allowing him to seek me, find me and caress me with tenderness. The question put to us simply by the Infant's presence is: do I allow God to love me?

More so, do we have the courage to welcome with tenderness the difficulties and problems of those who are near to us, or do we prefer impersonal solutions, perhaps effective but devoid of the warmth of the Gospel? How much the world needs tenderness today! The patience of God, the closeness of God, the tenderness of God.

The Christian response cannot be different from God's response to our smallness. Life must be met with goodness, with meekness. When we realise that God is in love with our smallness, that he made himself small in order to better encounter us, we cannot help but open our hearts to him, and beseech him: 'Lord, help me to be like you, give me the grace of tenderness in the most difficult circumstances of life, give me the grace of closeness in the face of every need, of meekness in every conflict'.

Dear brothers and sisters, on this holy night we contemplate the nativity scene: there 'the people who walked in darkness have seen a great light' (Is 9:1). People who were unassuming, people open to receiving the gift of God, were the ones who saw this light. This light was not seen, however, by the arrogant, the proud, by those who made laws according to their own personal measures, who were closed off to others. Let us look to the crib and pray, asking the Blessed Mother: 'O Mary, show us Jesus!'.

Vatican Basilica, Wednesday, 24 December 2014

'All Sadness Has Been Banished'

TONIGHT 'A GREAT LIGHT' SHINES FORTH
(Is 9:1); the light of Jesus' birth shines all about
us. How true and timely are the words of the
prophet Isaiah which we have just heard: 'You
have brought abundant joy and great rejoicing'
(9:2)! Our heart was already joyful in awaiting this
moment; now that joy abounds and overflows,
for the promise has been at last fulfilled. Joy
and gladness are a sure sign that the message
contained in the mystery of this night is truly
from God. There is no room for doubt; let us leave
that to the skeptics who, by looking to reason
alone, never find the truth. There is no room for
the indifference which reigns in the hearts of

those unable to love for fear of losing something. All sadness has been banished, for the Child Jesus brings true comfort to every heart.

Today, the Son of God is born, and everything changes. The Saviour of the world comes to partake of our human nature; no longer are we alone and forsaken. The Virgin offers us her Son as the beginning of a new life. The true light has come to illumine our lives so often beset by the darkness of sin. Today we once more discover who we are! Tonight we have been shown the way to reach the journey's end. Now must we put away all fear and dread, for the light shows us the path to Bethlehem. We must not be laggards; we are not permitted to stand idle. We must set out to see our Saviour lying in a manger. This is the reason for our joy and gladness: this Child has been 'born to us'; he was 'given to us', as Isaiah proclaims (cf. 9:5). The people who for two thousand years has traversed all the pathways of the world in order to allow every man and woman to share in this joy is now given the mission of making known 'the Prince of Peace' and becoming his effective servant in the midst of the nations.

So when we hear tell of the birth of Christ, let us be silent and let the Child speak. Let us take his words to heart in rapt contemplation of his face. If we take him in our arms and let ourselves be embraced by him, he will bring us unending peace of heart. This Child teaches us what is truly essential in our lives. He was born into the poverty of this world; there was no room in the inn for him and his family. He found shelter and support in a stable and was laid in a manger for animals. And yet, from this nothingness, the light of God's glory shines forth. From now on, the way of authentic liberation and perennial redemption is open to every man and woman who is simple of heart. This Child, whose face radiates the goodness, mercy and love of God the Father, trains us, his disciples, as St Paul says, 'to reject godless ways' and the richness of the world, in order to live 'temperately, justly and devoutly' (Tit 2:12).

In a society so often intoxicated by consumerism and hedonism, wealth and extravagance, appearances and narcissism, this Child calls us to act *soberly*, in other words, in a way that is simple, balanced, consistent, capable of seeing and doing what is essential. In a world which all too often is merciless to the sinner and lenient to the sin, we need to cultivate a strong sense of justice, to discern and to do God's will. Amid a culture of indifference which not infrequently turns ruthless, our style of life should instead be *devout*, filled with empathy, compassion and mercy, drawn daily from the wellspring of prayer.

Like the shepherds of Bethlehem, may we too, with eyes full of amazement and wonder, gaze upon the Child Jesus, the Son of God. And in his presence may our hearts burst forth in prayer: 'Show us, Lord, your mercy, and grant us your salvation' (Ps 85:8).

Vatican Basilica, Thursday, 24 December 2015

'A Child Has Been Born to Us'

'THE GRACE OF GOD HAS APPEARED,
bringing salvation to all' (Tit 2:11). The words of
the Apostle Paul reveal the mystery of this holy
night: the grace of God has appeared, his free gift.
In the Child given to us, the love of God is made
visible.

It is a *night of glory*, that glory proclaimed by the
angels in Bethlehem and by ourselves as well,
all over the world. It is a *night of joy*, because
henceforth and for ever, the infinite and eternal
God is *God with us*. He is not far off. We need
not search for him in the heavens or in mystical
notions. He is close at hand. He became man and
he will never withdraw from our humanity, which

he has made his own. It is a *night of light*. The light prophesied by Isaiah (cf. 9:1), which was to shine on those who walked in a land of darkness, has appeared and enveloped the shepherds of Bethlehem (cf. Lk 2:9).

The shepherds discover simply that 'a child has been born to us' (Is 9:5). They realise that all this glory, all this joy, all this light, converges to a single point, the *sign* that the angel indicated to them: 'You will find a child wrapped in swaddling clothes and lying in a manger' (Lk 2:12). This is *the enduring sign* for all who would find Jesus. Not just then, but also today. If we want to celebrate Christmas authentically, we need to contemplate this sign: the frail simplicity of a tiny newborn child, the meekness with which he is placed in a manger, the tender affection with which he is wrapped in his swaddling clothes. That is where God is.

With this sign, the Gospel reveals a paradox. It speaks of the emperor, the governor, the high and mighty of those times, yet God does not make himself present there. He appears not in the splendour of a royal palace, but in the poverty of a stable; not in pomp and show, but in simplicity of life; not in power, but in astonishing smallness. In order to meet him, we need to go where he is. We need to bow down, to humble ourselves, to make ourselves small. The newborn Child challenges us. He calls us to leave behind fleeting illusions and to turn to what is essential, to renounce our insatiable cravings, to abandon our endless yearning for things we will never have. We do well to leave such things behind, in order to discover, in the simplicity of the divine Child, peace, joy and the luminous meaning of life.

Let us allow the Child in the manger to challenge us, but let us also be challenged by all those children in today's world who are lying not in a crib, caressed with affection by their mothers and fathers, but in squalid 'mangers that devour dignity'. Children who hide underground to escape bombardment, on the pavements of large cities, in the hold of a boat overladen with immigrants … Let us allow ourselves to be challenged by those children who are not allowed to be born, by those who cry because no one relieves their hunger, by those who hold in their hands not toys, but weapons.

The mystery of Christmas, which is light and joy, challenges and unsettles us, because it is at once a *mystery of hope and of sadness*. It has a *taste of sadness*, inasmuch as love is not accepted, and life discarded. Such was the case with Joseph and Mary, who met with closed doors, and placed Jesus in a manger, 'because there was no place for them in the inn' (2:7). Jesus was born rejected by some and regarded by many others with indifference. Today too, that same indifference can exist, whenever Christmas becomes a holiday with ourselves at the centre rather than Jesus; when the lights of shop windows push the light of God into the shadows; when we are enthused about gifts but indifferent to our neighbours in need. This worldliness has kidnapped Christmas; we need to liberate it!

Yet Christmas has above all a *taste of hope* because, for all the darkness in our lives, God's light shines forth. His gentle light does not frighten us. God, who is in love with us, draws us to himself with his tenderness, by being born poor and frail in our midst, as one of us. He is born in Bethlehem, which means 'house of bread'. In this way, he seems to tell us that he is born as *bread for us*; he enters our life to give us his life; he comes into our world to give us his love. He does not come to devour or to lord it over us, but instead to feed and serve us. There is a straight line between the manger and the cross where Jesus will become *bread that is broken*. It is the straight line of love that gives and saves, the love that brings light to our lives and peace to our hearts.

That night, the shepherds understood this. They were among the marginalised of those times. Yet no one is marginalised in the sight of God, and that Christmas, they themselves were the guests. People who felt sure of themselves, self-sufficient, were at home with their possessions.

It was the shepherds who 'set out with haste' (Lk 2:16). Tonight, may we too be challenged and called by Jesus. Let us approach him with trust, starting from all those things that make us feel marginalised, from our limitations and our sins. Let us be touched by the tenderness that saves. Let us draw close to God who draws close to us. Let us pause to gaze upon the crib, and relive in our imagination the birth of Jesus: light and peace, dire poverty and rejection. With the shepherds, let us enter into the real Christmas, bringing to Jesus all that we are, our alienation, our unhealed wounds, our sins. Then, in Jesus, we will enjoy the taste of the true spirit of Christmas: the beauty of being loved by God. With Mary and Joseph, let us pause before the manger, before Jesus who is born as bread for my life. Contemplating his humble and infinite love, let us simply tell him: Thank you. Thank you because you have done all this *for me*.

Vatican Basilica, Saturday, 24 December 2016

PART II:
General Audiences of Pope Francis

'We Need Not Be Afraid'

Dear brothers and sisters, good morning!

Today I would like to begin the last series of catecheses on our profession of faith, by discussing the statement 'I believe in eternal life'. In particular, I will reflect on the Last Judgement. We need not be afraid: let us listen to what the Word of God tells us. Concerning this, we read in the Gospel of Matthew: when Christ 'comes in his glory, and all the angels with him … Before him will be gathered all the nations, and he will separate them one from another as a shepherd separates the sheep from the goats, and he will place the sheep at his right hand, but the goats at the left … And they will go away into eternal punishment, but the righteous into eternal life' (Mt 25:31-33, 46). Whenever we think of Christ's return and of his final judgement, which will manifest to its ultimate consequences the good that each person has done or failed to do during his earthly life, we seem to find ourselves before a mystery which towers above us, which we fail even to imagine. A mystery which almost instinctively arouses a sense of fear in us, and perhaps even one of trepidation. If, however, we reflect well on this reality, it cannot but expand the heart of a Christian and come to constitute a cause of consolation and of trust.

In this regard, the testimony of the first Christian communities resounds ever so evocatively. In fact, they usually accompanied the celebrations and prayers with the acclamation *Maranatha*, an expression composed of two Aramaic words which, according to how they are pronounced, may be understood as a supplication: 'Come, Lord!', or as a certainty nourished by faith:

'Yes, the Lord is coming, the Lord is near'. The whole of Christian revelation culminates in this exclamation, at the conclusion of the marvellous contemplation which is offered to us by John in Revelation (cf. 22:20). In that case, it is the Church as bride who, on behalf of all humanity and as its first fruits, addresses herself to Christ her Bridegroom, looking forward to be enfolded in his embrace: Jesus' embrace, which is the fullness of life and the fullness of love. This is how Jesus embraces us. If we think of judgement in this perspective, all fear and hesitation fade and make room for expectation and deep joy: it will be the very moment when we will be judged finally ready to be clothed in Christ's glory, as with a nuptial garment, to be led into the banquet, the image of full and definitive communion with God.

A second reason for confidence is offered to us by the observation that, at the moment of judgement, *we will not be left alone*. In the Gospel of Matthew, Jesus himself foretells how, at the end of time, those who have followed him will take their place in glory, and judge with him (cf. Mt 19:28). The Apostle Paul then, writing to the community of Corinth, states: 'Do you not know that the saints will judge the world?… How much more, matters pertaining to this life!' (1 Cor 6:2-3). How beautiful it is to know that at that juncture, in addition to Christ, our Paraclete, our Advocate with the Father (cf. 1 Jn 2:1), we will be able to count on the intercession and goodness of so many of our elder brothers and sisters who have gone before us on the journey of faith, who have offered their lives for us and who continue to love us ineffably! The saints already live in the sight of God, in the splendour of his glory praying for us who still live on earth. What consolation this certainty arouses in our hearts! The Church is truly a mother and, as a mother, she seeks her children's good, especially of those who are furthest away and are afflicted, until she finds its fullness in the glorious body of Christ with all its members.

A further suggestion is offered to us by the Gospel of John, where it explicitly states that 'God sent

his Son into the world, not to condemn the
world, but that the world might be saved through
him. He who believes in him is not condemned;
he who does not believe is condemned already,
because he has not believed in the name of the
only Son of God' (Jn 3:17-18). This means, then,
that *this final judgement is already in progress*, it
begins now over the course of our lives. Thus
judgement is pronounced at every moment of life,
as it sums up our faith in the salvation which is
present and active in Christ, or of our unbelief,
whereby we close in upon ourselves. But if we
close ourselves to the love of Jesus, we condemn
ourselves. Salvation is to open oneself to Jesus, it is
he who saves us. If we are sinners – and we all are
– we ask him for forgiveness and if we go to him
with the desire to be good, the Lord forgives us.
But for this we must open ourselves to Jesus' love,
which is stronger than all else. Jesus' love is great,
Jesus' love is merciful, Jesus' love forgives; but you
have to open yourself and to open oneself means
to repent, to accuse oneself of the things that are
not good and which we have done. The Lord Jesus

gave himself and he continues to give himself to us, in order to fill us with all of the mercy and grace of the Father. We then, in a certain sense, can become judges of ourselves, by condemning ourselves to exclusion from communion with God and with the brethren. We must not grow weary, then, of keeping watch over our thoughts and our attitudes, in order that we may be given even now a foretaste of the warmth and splendour of God's Face – and this will be beautiful – which in eternal life we shall contemplate in all its fullness. Forward, thinking of this judgement which begins now, which has already begun; forward, doing so in such a way that our hearts open to Jesus and to his salvation; forward without fear, for Jesus' love is greater and if we ask forgiveness for our sins he will forgive us. This is what Jesus is like. Forward then with this certainly, which will bring us to the glory of heaven!

St Peter's Square, Wednesday, 11 December 2013

'God the Father is Generous'

Dear brothers and sisters, good morning!

Our meeting is taking place in the spiritual climate of Advent, which is made all the more intense by the Holy Christmas Novena we are experiencing in these days that lead us to the celebration of Christmas. Therefore, today I would like to reflect with you on the Birth of Jesus, the feast of trust and of hope which overcomes uncertainty and pessimism. And the reason for our hope is this: God is with us and God still trusts us! Think well on this: God is with us and God still trusts us. God the Father is generous. He comes to abide with mankind, he chooses earth as his dwelling place to remain with people and to be found where man passes his days in joy or in sorrow. Therefore, earth is no longer only 'a valley of tears'; rather, it is the place where God himself has pitched his tent, it is the meeting place of God with man, of God's solidarity with men.

God willed to share in our human condition to the point of becoming one with us in the Person of Jesus, who is true Man and true God. However, there is something even more surprising. The presence of God among men did not take place in a perfect, idyllic world but rather in this real world, which is marked by so many things both good and bad, by division, wickedness, poverty, arrogance and war. He chose to live in our history as it is, with all the weight of its limitations and of its tragedies. In doing so, he has demonstrated in an unequalled manner his merciful and truly loving disposition toward the human creature. He is God-with-us. Jesus is God-with-us. Do you believe this? Together let us profess: Jesus is God with us! Jesus is God with us always and for ever with us in history's suffering and sorrow. The Birth of Jesus reveals that God 'sided' with man once and for all, to save us, to raise us from the dust of our misery, from our difficulty, from our sins.

Hence the great 'gift' of the Child of Bethlehem: He brings us a spiritual energy, an energy which helps us not to despair in our struggle, in our hopelessness, in our sadness, for it is an energy that warms and transforms the heart. Indeed, the Birth of Jesus brings us the Good News that we are loved immensely and uniquely by God, and he not only enables us to know this love, he also gives it to us, he communicates it to us!

We may derive two considerations from the joyous contemplation of the mystery of the Son of God born for us.

The first is that if God, in the Christmas mystery, reveals himself not as One who remains on high and dominates the universe, but as the One who bends down, descends to the little and poor earth, it means that, to be like him, we should not put ourselves above others, but indeed lower ourselves, place ourselves at the service of others, become small with the small and poor with the poor. It is regrettable to see a Christian who does not want to lower himself, who does not want to serve. A Christian who struts about is ugly: this is not Christian, it is pagan. The Christian serves, he lowers himself. Let us be sure that our brothers and sisters do not ever feel alone!

The second consequence: if God, through Jesus, involved himself with man to the point of becoming one of us, it means that whatever we have done to a brother or a sister we have done to him. Jesus himself reminded us of this: whoever has fed, welcomed, visited, loved one of the least and poorest of men, will have done it to the Son of God.

Let us entrust ourselves to the maternal intercession of Mary, the Mother of Jesus and our Mother, that she may help us this holy Christmastide, which is already close at hand, to see in the face of our neighbour, especially the weakest and most marginalised people, the image of the Son of God made man.

St Peter's Square, Wednesday, 18 December 2013

'Jesus was Born in a Family'

Dear brothers and sisters, good morning!

The Synod of Bishops on the Family, recently celebrated, was the first stage of a journey, which will conclude next October with the celebration of another Assembly on the theme: 'The Vocation and Mission of the Family in the Church and [Contemporary] World'. The prayer and reflection which must accompany this journey is required of all the People of God. I would also like the customary meditations of the Wednesday Audiences to be included in this common journey. I have therefore decided to reflect with you, this year, precisely on the family, on this great gift that the Lord has made to the world from the very beginning, when he entrusted Adam and Eve with the mission to multiply and fill the earth (cf. Gen 1:28); that gift that Jesus confirmed and sealed in his Gospel.

The nearness of Christmas casts a great light on this mystery. The Incarnation of the Son of God opens a new beginning in the universal history of man and woman. And this new beginning happens within a family, in Nazareth. Jesus was born in a family. He could have come in a spectacular way, or as a warrior, an emperor... No, no: he is born in a family, in a family. This is important: to perceive in the nativity, this beautiful scene.

God chose to come into the world in a human family, which He himself formed. He formed it in a remote village on the outskirts of the Roman Empire. Not in Rome, which was the capital of the Empire, not in a big city, but on its nearly invisible outskirts, indeed, of little renown. The

Gospels also recall this, almost as an expression: 'Can anything good come out of Nazareth?' (Jn 1:46). Perhaps, in many parts of the world, we still talk this way, when we hear the name of some areas on the periphery of a big city. And so, right there, on the outskirts of the great Empire, began the most holy and good story of Jesus among men! And that is where this family was.

Jesus dwelt on that periphery for thirty years. The evangelist Luke summarises this period like this: Jesus 'was obedient to them' – that is, to Mary and Joseph. And someone might say: 'But did this God, who comes to save us, waste thirty years there, in that suburban slum?'. He wasted thirty years! He wanted this. Jesus' path was in that family – 'and his mother kept all these things in her heart. And Jesus increased in wisdom and in stature, and in favour with God and man' (Lk 2:51-52). It does not recount miracles or healing, or preaching – He did none in that period – or of crowds flocking; in Nazareth everything seemed to happen 'normally', according to the customs of a pious and hardworking Israelite family: they worked, the mother cooked, she did all the housework, ironed shirts … all the things mothers do. The father, a carpenter, worked, taught his son the trade. Thirty years. 'But what a waste, Father!' God works in mysterious ways. But what was important there was the family! And this was not a waste! They were great saints: Mary, the most holy woman, immaculate, and Joseph, a most righteous man… the family.

We are certainly moved by the story of how the adolescent Jesus followed the religious calendar of the community and the social duties; in knowing how, as a young worker, he worked with Joseph; and then how he attended the reading of the Scriptures, in praying the Psalms and in so many other customs of daily life. The Gospels, in their sobriety, make no reference to Jesus' adolescence and leave this task to our loving meditation. Art, literature, music have taken this journey through imagination. It is certainly not difficult to imagine how much mothers could learn from Mary's care

for that Son! And how much fathers could glean
from the example of Joseph, a righteous man, who
dedicated his life to supporting and protecting the
Child and his wife – his family – in difficult times.
Not to mention how much children could be
encouraged by the adolescent Jesus to understand
the necessity and beauty of cultivating their
most profound vocation and of dreaming great
dreams! In those thirty years, Jesus cultivated his
vocation, for which the Father had sent him. And
in that time, Jesus never became discouraged, but
increased in courage in order to carry his mission
forward.

Each Christian family can first of all – as Mary
and Joseph did – welcome Jesus, listen to him,
speak with him, guard him, protect him, grow
with him; and in this way improve the world. Let
us make room in our heart and in our day for the
Lord. As Mary and Joseph also did, and it was not
easy: how many difficulties they had to overcome!
They were not a superficial family, they were not
an unreal family. The family of Nazareth urges

us to rediscover the vocation and mission of the family, of every family. And, what happened in those thirty years in Nazareth, can thus happen to us too: in seeking to make love and not hate normal, making mutual help commonplace, not indifference or enmity. It is no coincidence, then, that 'Nazareth' means 'She who keeps', as Mary, who – as the Gospel states – 'kept all these things in her heart' (cf. Lk 2:19, 51). Since then, each time there is a family that keeps this mystery, even if it were on the periphery of the world, the mystery of the Son of God, the mystery of Jesus who comes to save us, the mystery is at work. He comes to save the world. And this is the great mission of the family: to make room for Jesus who is coming, to welcome Jesus in the family, in each member: children, husband, wife, grandparents … Jesus is there. Welcome him there, in order that he grow spiritually in the family. May the Lord grant us this grace in these last days of Advent. Thank you.

St Peter's Square, Wednesday, 17 December 2014

'He is the Font of Love and Serenity'

Dear brothers and sisters, good morning!

In these days of Christmas the Child Jesus is placed before us. I am certain that in our homes many families still have a nativity scene arranged, continuing this beautiful tradition brought about by St Francis of Assisi which keeps alive in our hearts the mystery of God who became man.

Devotion to the Child Jesus is widespread. Many saints cultivated this devotion in their daily prayers, and wished to model their lives after that of the Child Jesus. I think in particular of St Thérèse of Lisieux, who as a Carmelite nun took the name Thérèse of the Child Jesus

and the Holy Face. She is also a Doctor of the
Church who knew how to live and witness to the
'spiritual childhood' which is assimilated through
meditation, as the Virgin Mary taught, on the
humility of God who became small for us. This
is a great mystery. God is humble! We, who are
proud and full of vanity, believe we are something
big: we are nothing! He, the Great One, is humble
and becomes a child. This is a true mystery. God is
humble. This is beautiful!

There was a time in which, in the divine-human
Person of Christ, God was a child, and this
must hold a particular significance for our faith.
It is true that his death on the cross and his
Resurrection are the highest expressions of his
redeeming love, however let us not forget that
the whole of his earthly life is revelation and
teaching. In the Christmas season we remember
his childhood. In order to grow in faith we will
need to contemplate the Child Jesus more often.
Certainly, we know nothing of this period of his
life. The rare indications that we possess refer to

the imposition of his name eight days after his birth and his presentation at the Temple (cf. Lk 2:21-28); in addition to this, the visit of the Magi and the ensuing escape to Egypt (cf. Mt 2:1-23). Then, there is a great leap to twelve years of age, when with Mary and Joseph he goes in pilgrimage to Jerusalem for Passover, and instead of returning with his parents, he remains in the Temple to speak with the doctors of the law.

As we see, we know little of the Child Jesus, but we can learn much about him if we look to the lives of children. It is a beautiful habit that parents and grandparents have, that of watching what the children do.

We discover, first of all, that children want our attention. They have to be at the centre – why? Because they are proud? No! Because they need to feel protected. It is important that we too place Jesus at the centre of our life and know, even if it may seem paradoxical, that it is our responsibility to protect him. He wants to be in our embrace, he wants to be tended to and to be able to fix his gaze on ours. Additionally, we must make the Child Jesus smile in order to show him our love and our joy that he is in our midst. His smile is a sign of the love that gives us the assurance of being loved. Children, lastly, love to play. Playing with children, however, means abandoning our logic in order to enter theirs. If we want to have fun it is necessary to understand what they like, and not to be selfish and make them do the things that we like. It is a lesson for us. Before Jesus we are called to abandon our pretense of autonomy – and this is the crux of the matter: our pretense of autonomy – in order to instead accept the true form of liberty, which consists in knowing and serving whom we have before us. He, the Child, is the Son of God who comes to save us. He has come among us to show us the face of the Father abounding in love and mercy. Therefore, let us hold the Child Jesus tightly in our arms; let us place ourselves at his service. He is the font of love and serenity. It will be beautiful today, when we get home, to go to the nativity scene and kiss the

Baby Jesus and say: 'Jesus, I want to be humble like you, humble like God', and to ask him for this grace.

St Peter's Square, Wednesday, 30 December 2015

'Comfort, Comfort My People ...'

Dear brothers and sisters, good morning!

Today we shall begin a new series of catecheses, on the theme of *Christian hope*. It is very important, because hope never disappoints. Optimism disappoints, but hope does not! We have such need, in these times which appear dark, in which we sometimes feel disoriented at the evil and violence which surrounds us, at the distress of so many of our brothers and sisters. We need hope! We feel disoriented and even rather discouraged, because we are powerless and it seems this darkness will never end.

We must not let hope abandon us, because God, with his love, walks with us. 'I hope, because God is beside me': we can all say this. Each one of us can say: 'I hope, I have hope, because God walks with me'. He walks and he holds my hand. God does not leave us to ourselves. The Lord Jesus has conquered evil and has opened the path of life for us.

Thus, particularly in this Season of Advent, which is the time of waiting, in which we prepare ourselves to welcome once again the comforting mystery of the Incarnation and the light of Christmas, it is important to reflect on hope. Let us allow the Lord to teach us what it means to hope. Therefore let us listen to the words of Sacred Scripture, beginning with *the Prophet Isaiah*, the great Prophet of Advent, the great messenger of hope.

In the second part of his Book, Isaiah addresses the people with his *message of comfort*:

Comfort, comfort my people, says your God.
Speak tenderly to Jerusalem, and cry to her
that her warfare is ended, that her iniquity is
pardoned...

A voice cries: 'In the wilderness prepare the
way of the Lord, make straight in the desert
a highway for our God. Every valley shall be
lifted up, and every mountain and hill be made
low; the uneven ground shall become level,
and the rough places a plain. And the glory of
the Lord shall be revealed, and all flesh shall
see it together, for the mouth of the Lord has
spoken'. (40:1-2, 3-5).

God the Father comforts by raising up comforters,
whom he asks to encourage the people, his
children, by proclaiming that the tribulation has
ended, affliction has ended, and sins have been
forgiven. This is what heals the afflicted and
fearful heart. This is why the Prophet asks them to
prepare the way of the Lord, to be ready to receive
his gifts and his salvation.

For the people, comfort begins with the opportunity to walk on God's path, a new path, made straight and passable, a way prepared *in the desert*, so as to make it possible to cross it and return to the homeland. The Prophet addresses the people who are living the tragedy of the Exile in Babylon, and now instead they hear that they may return to their land, across a path made smooth and wide, without valleys and mountains that make the journey arduous, a level path across the desert. Thus, preparing that path means preparing *a way of salvation and liberation* from every obstacle and hindrance.

The Exile was a fraught moment in the history of Israel, when the people had lost everything. The people had lost their homeland, freedom, dignity, and even trust in God. They felt abandoned and hopeless. Instead, however, there is the Prophet's appeal which reopens the heart to faith. *The desert* is a place in which it is difficult to live, but precisely there, one can now walk in order to *return not only to the homeland, but return to God, and return to hoping and smiling.* When we are in darkness, in difficulty, we do not smile, and it is precisely hope which teaches us to smile in order to find the path that leads to God. One of the first things that happens to people who distance themselves from God is that they are people who do not smile. Perhaps they can break into a loud laugh, one after another, a joke, a chuckle … but their smile is missing! Only hope brings a smile: it is the hopeful smile in the expectation of finding God.

Life is often a desert, it is difficult to walk in life, but if we trust in God it can become beautiful and wide as a highway. Just never lose hope, just continue to believe, always, in spite of everything. When we are before a child, although we have many problems and many difficulties, a smile comes to us from within, because we see hope in front of us: a child is hope! And in this way we must be able to discern in life the way of hope which leads us to find God, God who became a Child for us. He will make us smile, he will give us everything!

These very words of Isaiah were then used by John the Baptist in his preaching that invites to conversion. This is what he said: 'The voice of one crying in the wilderness: Prepare the way of the Lord' (Mt 3:3). It is a voice which cries out where it seems that no one can hear it – for who can listen in the desert? – and which cries out in the disorientation caused by a crisis of faith. We cannot deny that the world today is in a crisis of faith. One says: 'I believe in God, I am a Christian' – 'I belong to this religion…'. But your life is far from being Christian; it is far removed from God! Religion, faith is but an expression: 'Do I believe?' – 'Yes!'. This means returning to God, converting the heart to God and going on this path to find him. He is waiting for us. This is John the Baptist's preaching: prepare. Prepare for the encounter with this Child who will give our smile back to us. When the Baptist proclaims Jesus' coming, it is as if the Israelites are still in exile, because they are under the Roman dominion, which renders them foreigners in their own homeland, ruled by powerful occupiers that make decisions about their lives. However, the true history is not the one made by the powerful, but the one *made by God together with his little ones.* The true history – that which will remain in eternity – is the one that God writes *with his little ones*: God with Mary, God with Jesus, God with Joseph, *God with the little ones.* Those little and simple people whom we see around the newborn Jesus: Zechariah and Elizabeth, who were old and barren, Mary, the young virgin maiden betrothed to Joseph, the shepherds, who were scorned and counted for nothing. It is the little ones, made great by their faith, *the little ones who are able to continue to hope.* Hope is the virtue of the *little ones.* The great ones, those who are satisfied, do not know hope; they do not know what it is.

It is the little ones with God, with Jesus, who transform the desert of exile, of desperation and loneliness, of suffering, into a level plain on which to walk in order to encounter the glory of the Lord. We have come to the 'point': let us be taught hope. Let us be confident as we await the coming of the Lord, and what the desert may represent in our life – each one knows what desert he or she is walking in – it will become a garden in bloom. Hope does not disappoint!

Paul VI Audience Hall
Wednesday, 7 December 2016

'He Who Brings Peace'

Dear brothers and sisters, good morning!

We are coming close to Christmas, and the prophet Isaiah once again helps us to open ourselves to the hope of welcoming the Good News of the coming of salvation.

Isaiah 52 begins with the invitation addressed to Jerusalem to awake, shake off the dust and chains, and put on the most beautiful clothes, because the Lord has come to free his people (1-3). And he adds: 'my people shall know my name; therefore in that day they shall know that it is I who speak; here am I' (6). It is to this 'here am I' said by the Lord, which sums up his firm will for salvation and closeness to us, that Jerusalem responds with a song of joy, according to the prophet's invitation. It is a very important historic moment. It is the end of the Babylonian Exile; it is the opportunity for Israel to rediscover God and, in faith, rediscover itself. The Lord is near, and the 'remnant', that is, the small population which survived the Exile and whose faith endured while in exile, which had undergone crises and continued to believe and hope even in the midst of darkness, that 'remnant' will be able to see the wonders of God.

At this point, the prophet includes a song of exaltation:

> How beautiful upon the mountains are the
> feet of him who brings good tidings,
> who publishes peace, who brings good tidings
> of good,
> who publishes salvation,
> who says to Zion, 'Your God reigns' ….
> Break forth together into singing, you waste

places of Jerusalem;
for the Lord has comforted his people,
he has redeemed Jerusalem.
The Lord has bared his holy arm before the
eyes of all the nations;
and all the ends of the earth shall see the
salvation of our God' (Is 52:7, 9-10).

These words of Isaiah, upon which we want to
linger a while, make reference to the miracle of
peace, and do so in a very specific way, placing the
gaze not on the messenger but on his feet which
are running quickly: 'How beautiful upon the
mountains are the feet of him who brings good
tidings …'

He is like the spouse in the Canticle of Canticles
who runs towards his beloved: 'Behold, he comes,
leaping upon the mountains, bounding over the
hills' (Cant 2:8). Thus, even the messenger of
peace runs, bringing the happy announcement of
liberation, of salvation, and proclaiming that God
reigns.

God has not abandoned his people, and he has not left them to be vanquished by evil, because he is faithful, and his grace is greater than sin. We must learn this, because we are stubborn and do not learn. However, I ask: what is greater, God or sin? God! And which is victorious to the end? God or sin? God. Is he able to defeat the most serious, most shameful, the most terrible sin, the worst of sins? With what weapon does God defeat sin? With love! This means that 'God reigns'; these are the words of faith in a Lord whose power bends down to humanity, stoops down, to offer mercy and to free man and woman from all that disfigures in them the beautiful image of God, for when we are in sin, God's image is disfigured. The fulfillment of so much love will be the very Kingdom instituted by Jesus, that Kingdom of forgiveness and peace which we celebrate at Christmas, and which is definitively achieved at Easter. And the most beautiful joy of Christmas is that interior joy of peace: the Lord has remitted my sins, the Lord has forgiven me, the Lord has had mercy on me, he came to save me. This is the joy of Christmas!

These are, brothers and sisters, the reasons for our hope. When everything seems finished, when, faced with many negative realities, and faith becomes demanding, and there comes the temptation which says that nothing makes sense anymore, behold instead the beautiful news brought by those swift feet: God is coming to fulfil something new, to establish a Kingdom of Peace. God has 'bared his arm' and comes to bring freedom and consolation. Evil will not triumph forever; there is an end to suffering. Despair is defeated because God is among us.

And we too are urged to awake a little, like Jerusalem, according to the invitation of the prophet; we are called to become men and women of hope, cooperating in the coming of this Kingdom made of light and destined for all, men and women of hope. How bad is it when we find a Christian who has lost hope! 'But, I don't hope in anything; everything is finished for me': thus says a Christian who is incapable of looking to the horizons of hope, and before whose heart there is only a wall. However, God destroys such walls with forgiveness! And for this reason we must pray, that each day God may give us hope and give it to everyone: that hope which arises when we see God in the crib in Bethlehem. The message of the Good News entrusted to us is urgent. We too must run like the messenger on the mountains, because the world cannot wait, humanity is hungry and thirsty for justice, truth, peace.

And seeing the little Child of Bethlehem, the little ones of the world will know that the promise was accomplished; the message is fulfilled. In a newborn baby, in need of everything, wrapped in swaddling clothes and laid in a manger, there is enclosed all of the power of God who saves. Christmas is a day which opens the heart: we need to open our heart to this littleness which is there in that Child, and to that great wonder. It is the wonder of Christmas, for which we are preparing, with hope, in this Season of Advent. It is the surprise of a Child God, of a poor God, of a

weak God, of a God who abandons his greatness
to come close to each one of us.

Paul VI Audience Hall
Wednesday, 14 December 2016

'Christ's Birth is the Source of Hope'

Dear brothers and sisters, good morning!

We have recently begun a catechetical journey on the theme of hope, which is so very appropriate in the Season of Advent. The Prophet Isaiah has guided us up to this point. Today, just days before Christmas, I would like to reflect more specifically on the moment in which, so to speak, *hope came into the world*, with the incarnation of the Son of God. It was also Isaiah who foretold the birth of the Messiah in several passages: 'Behold, a young woman shall conceive and bear a son, and shall call his name Immanuel' (7:14); and also: 'there shall come forth a shoot from the stump of Jesse, and a branch shall grow out of his roots' (11:1). In these passages, the meaning of Christmas shines through: God fulfils the promise by becoming man; not abandoning his people, he draws near to the point of stripping himself of his divinity. In this way God shows his fidelity and inaugurates a new Kingdom, which gives *a new hope to mankind*. And what is this hope? Eternal life.

When we speak of hope, often it refers to what is not in man's power to realise, which is invisible. In fact, what we hope for goes beyond our strength and our perception. But the Birth of Christ, inaugurating redemption, speaks to us of a different hope, a dependable, visible and understandable hope, because it is founded in God. He comes into the world and gives us the strength to walk with him: God walks with us in Jesus, and walking with him toward the fullness of life gives us the strength to dwell in the present in a new, albeit arduous, way. Thus for a Christian, to hope means the certainty of being on a journey with Christ toward the Father who awaits us. Hope is never still; hope is always journeying, and it makes us journey. This hope, which the Child of Bethlehem gives us, offers a destination, a sure, ongoing goal, salvation of mankind, blessedness to those who trust in a merciful God. Saint Paul summarises all this with the expression: 'in this hope we were saved' (Rom 8:24). In other words, walking in this world, with hope, we are saved. Here we can ask ourselves the question, each one of us: am I walking with hope or is my interior life static, closed? Is my heart a locked drawer or a drawer open to the hope which enables me to walk – not alone – with Jesus?

In Christian homes, during the Season of Advent, *the nativity scene* is arranged, according to the tradition which dates back to St Francis of Assisi. In its simple way, the nativity scene conveys hope; each one of the characters is immersed in this atmosphere of hope.

First of all we note the place in which Jesus was born: *Bethlehem*. A small village in Judea where, thousands of years earlier, David was born, the shepherd boy chosen by God to be the King of Israel. Bethlehem is not a capital city, and for this reason is preferred by divine Providence, who loves to act through the little ones and the humble. In that birthplace was born the highly anticipated 'Son of David', Jesus, in whom the hope of God and the hope of man meet.

Then we look to *Mary*, Mother of Hope. With her 'yes' she opened the door of our world to God: her maiden's heart was full of hope, wholly enlivened by faith; and thus God chose her and she believed in his word. She, who for nine months was the Ark of the new and eternal Covenant, in the grotto, contemplates the Child and sees in him the love of God, who comes to save his people and the whole of humanity.

Next to Mary is *Joseph*, a descendant of Jesse and of David; he too believed in the words of the angel, and looking at Jesus in the manger, reflects on the fact that that Child has come from the Holy Spirit, and that God himself commanded

him to call [the Child] 'Jesus'. In that name
there is hope for every man and woman, because
through that son of woman, God will save
mankind from death and from sin. This is why it is
important to contemplate the nativity scene!

In the nativity scene there are also *shepherds*,
who represent the humble and poor who await
the Messiah, the 'consolation of Israel' (Lk 2:25),
and the 'redemption of Jerusalem' (2:38). In this
Child they see the realisation of the promises
and hope that the salvation of God will finally
arrive for each of them. Those who trust in their
own certainties, especially material, do not await
God's salvation. Let us keep this in mind: our own
assurance will not save us; the only certainty that
will save us is that of hope in God. It will save us
because it is strong and enables us to journey in
life with joy, with the will to do good, with the
will to attain eternal happiness. The little ones, the
shepherds, instead trust in God, hope in him and
rejoice when they recognise in that Child the sign
indicated by the angels (cf. Lk 2:12).

The very *choir of angels* proclaims from on high the great design that the Child fulfills: 'Glory to God in the highest, and on earth peace among men with whom he is pleased' (2:14). Christian hope is expressed in praise and gratitude to God, who has initiated his Kingdom of love, justice and peace.

Dear brothers and sisters, in these days, contemplating the nativity scene, we prepare ourselves for the Birth of the Lord. It will truly be a celebration if we welcome Jesus, the seed of hope that God sets down in the furrows of our individual and community history. Every 'yes' to Jesus who comes, is a bud of hope. Let us trust in this bud of hope, in this 'yes': 'Yes, Jesus, you can save me, you can save me'. Happy Christmas of hope to all!

Paul VI Audience Hall
Wednesday, 21 December 2016

PART III
'Urbi et Orbi' Messages of Pope Francis for 25 December

'Peace to Mankind'

Dear brothers and sisters in Rome and throughout the whole world, greetings and happy Christmas!

I take up the song of the angels who appeared to the shepherds in Bethlehem on the night when Jesus was born. It is a song which unites heaven and earth, giving praise and glory to heaven, and the promise of peace to earth and all its people.

I ask everyone to share in this song: it is a song for every man or woman who keeps watch through the night, who hopes for a better world, who cares for others while humbly seeking to do his or her duty.

Glory to God!

Above all else, this is what Christmas bids us to do: give glory to God, for he is good, he is faithful, he is merciful. Today I voice my hope that everyone will come to know the true face of God, the Father who has given us Jesus. My hope is that everyone will feel God's closeness, live in his presence, love him and adore him.

May each of us give glory to God above all by our lives, by lives spent for love of him and of all our brothers and sisters.

Peace to mankind!

True peace – we know this well – is not a balance of opposing forces. It is not a lovely 'façade' which conceals conflicts and divisions. Peace calls for daily commitment, but making peace is an art, starting from God's gift, from the grace which he has given us in Jesus Christ.

Looking at the Child in the manger, Child of peace, our thoughts turn to those children who are the most vulnerable victims of wars, but we think too of the elderly, to battered women, to the sick ... Wars shatter and hurt so many lives!

Too many lives have been shattered in recent times by the conflict in Syria, fueling hatred and vengeance. Let us continue to ask the Lord to spare the beloved Syrian people further suffering, and to enable the parties in conflict to put an end to all violence and guarantee access to humanitarian aid. We have seen how powerful prayer is! And I am happy today too, that the followers of different religious confessions are joining us in our prayer for peace in Syria. Let us never lose the courage of prayer! The courage to say: Lord, grant your peace to Syria and to the whole world. And I also invite non-believers to desire peace with that yearning that makes the heart grow: all united, either by prayer or by desire. But all of us, for peace.

Grant peace, dear Child, to the Central African Republic, often forgotten and overlooked. Yet you, Lord, forget no one! And you also want to bring peace to that land, torn apart by a spiral of violence and poverty, where so many people are homeless, lacking water, food and the bare necessities of life. Foster social harmony in South Sudan, where current tensions have already caused too many victims and are threatening peaceful coexistence in that young state.

Prince of Peace, in every place turn hearts aside from violence and inspire them to lay down arms and undertake the path of dialogue. Look upon Nigeria, rent by constant attacks which do not spare the innocent and defenseless. Bless the land where you chose to come into the world, and grant a favourable outcome to the peace talks between Israelis and Palestinians. Heal the wounds of the beloved country of Iraq, once more struck by frequent acts of violence.

Lord of life, protect all who are persecuted for
your name. Grant hope and consolation to the
displaced and refugees, especially in the Horn of
Africa and in the eastern part of the Democratic
Republic of the Congo. Grant that migrants in
search of a dignified life may find acceptance
and assistance. May tragedies like those we
have witnessed this year, with so many deaths at
Lampedusa, never occur again!

Child of Bethlehem, touch the hearts of all those
engaged in human trafficking, that they may
realise the gravity of this crime against humanity.
Look upon the many children who are kidnapped,
wounded and killed in armed conflicts, and all
those who are robbed of their childhood and
forced to become soldiers.

Lord of heaven and earth, look upon our planet,
frequently exploited by human greed and rapacity.
Help and protect all the victims of natural
disasters, especially the beloved people of the
Philippines, gravely affected by the recent typhoon.

Dear brothers and sisters, today, in this world, in this humanity, is born the Saviour, who is Christ the Lord. Let us pause before the Child of Bethlehem. Let us allow our hearts to be touched, let us not fear this. Let us not fear that our hearts be moved. We need this! Let us allow ourselves to be warmed by the tenderness of God; we need his caress. God's caresses do not harm us. They give us peace and strength. We need his caresses. God is full of love: to him be praise and glory forever! God is peace: let us ask him to help us to be peacemakers each day, in our life, in our families, in our cities and nations, in the whole world. Let us allow ourselves to be moved by God's goodness.

❧

Christmas greetings after the Urbi et Orbi *Message:*

To you, dear brothers and sisters, gathered from throughout the world in this Square, and to all those from different countries who join us through the communications media, I offer my cordial best wishes for a merry Christmas!

On this day illumined by the Gospel hope which springs from the humble stable of Bethlehem, I invoke the Christmas gift of joy and peace upon all: upon children and the elderly, upon young people and families, the poor and the marginalised. May Jesus, who was born for us, console all those afflicted by illness and suffering; may he sustain those who devote themselves to serving our brothers and sisters who are most in need. Happy Christmas to all!

St Peter's Square, Wednesday, 25 December 2013

'Jesus is the Salvation'

Dear brothers and sisters, happy Christmas!

Jesus, the Son of God, the Saviour of the world, is born for us, born in Bethlehem of a Virgin, fulfilling the ancient prophecies. The Virgin's name is Mary, the wife of Joseph.

Humble people, full of hope in the goodness of God, are those who welcome Jesus and recognise him. And so the Holy Spirit enlightened the shepherds of Bethlehem, who hastened to the grotto and adored the Child. Then the Spirit led the elderly and humble couple Simeon and Anna into the temple of Jerusalem, and they recognised in Jesus the Messiah. 'My eyes have seen your salvation,' Simeon exclaimed, 'the salvation prepared by God in the sight of all peoples' (Lk 2:30).

Yes, brothers and sisters, Jesus is the salvation for every person and for every people!

Today I ask him, the Saviour of the world, to look upon our brothers and sisters in Iraq and Syria, who for too long now have suffered the effects of ongoing conflict, and who, together with those belonging to other ethnic and religious groups, are suffering a brutal persecution. May Christmas bring them hope, as indeed also to the many displaced persons, exiles and refugees, children, adults and elderly, from this region and from the whole world. May indifference be changed into closeness and rejection into hospitality, so that all who now are suffering may receive the necessary humanitarian help to overcome the rigours of winter, return to their countries and live with dignity. May the Lord open hearts to trust, and may he bestow his peace upon the whole Middle

East, beginning with the land blessed by his birth, thereby sustaining the efforts of those committed effectively to dialogue between Israelis and Palestinians.

May Jesus, Saviour of the world, protect all who suffer in Ukraine, and grant that their beloved land may overcome tensions, conquer hatred and violence, and set out on a new journey of fraternity and reconciliation.

May Christ the Saviour give peace to Nigeria, where [even in these hours] more blood is being shed and too many people are unjustly deprived of their possessions, held as hostages or killed. I invoke peace also on the other parts of the African continent, thinking especially of Libya, South Sudan, the Central African Republic, and various regions of the Democratic Republic of the Congo. I beseech all who have political responsibility to commit themselves through dialogue to overcoming differences and to building a lasting, fraternal coexistence.

May Jesus save the vast numbers of children who are victims of violence, made objects of trade and trafficking, or forced to become soldiers; children, so many abused children. May he give comfort to the families of the children killed in Pakistan last week. May he be close to all who suffer from illness, especially the victims of the Ebola epidemic, above all in Liberia, in Sierra Leone and in Guinea. As I thank all who are courageously dedicated to assisting the sick and their family members, I once more make an urgent appeal that the necessary assistance and treatment be provided.

The Child Jesus. My thoughts turn to all those children today who are killed and ill-treated, be they infants killed in the womb, deprived of that generous love of their parents and then buried in the egoism of a culture that does not love life; be they children displaced due to war and persecution, abused and taken advantage of before our very eyes and our complicit silence. I think also of those infants massacred in bomb attacks, also those where the Son of God was born. Even today, their impotent silence cries out under the sword of so many Herods. On their blood stands the shadow of contemporary Herods. Truly there are so many tears this Christmas, together with the tears of the Infant Jesus.

Dear brothers and sisters, may the Holy Spirit today enlighten our hearts, that we may recognise in the Infant Jesus, born in Bethlehem of the Virgin Mary, the salvation given by God to each one of us, to each man and woman and to all the peoples of the earth. May the power of Christ, which brings freedom and service, be felt in so many hearts afflicted by war, persecution and slavery. May this divine power, by its meekness, take away the hardness of heart of so many men and women immersed in worldliness and indifference, the globalisation of indifference. May his redeeming strength transform arms into ploughshares, destruction into creativity, hatred into love and tenderness. Then we will be able to cry out with joy: 'Our eyes have seen your salvation'.

With these thoughts I wish you all a happy Christmas!

St Peter's Square, Thursday, 25 December 2014

'Where God is Born, Hope is Born'

Dear brothers and sisters, happy Christmas!

Christ is born for us, *let us rejoice in the day of our salvation!*

Let us open our hearts to receive the grace of this day, which is Christ himself. Jesus is the radiant 'day' which has dawned on the horizon of humanity. A day of mercy, in which God our Father has revealed his great tenderness to the entire world. A day of light, which dispels the darkness of fear and anxiety. A day of peace, which makes for encounter, dialogue and, above all, reconciliation. A day of joy: a 'great joy' for the poor, the lowly and for all the people (cf. Lk 2:10).

On this day, Jesus, the Saviour is born of the Virgin Mary. The Crib makes us see the 'sign' which God has given us: 'a baby wrapped in swaddling cloths and lying in a manger' (Lk 2:12). Like the shepherds of Bethlehem, may we too set out to see this sign, this event which is renewed yearly in the Church. Christmas is an event which is renewed in every family, parish and community which receives the love of God made incarnate in Jesus Christ. Like Mary, the Church shows to everyone the 'sign' of God: the Child whom she bore in her womb and to whom she gave birth, yet who is the Son of the Most High, since he 'is of the Holy Spirit' (Mt 1:20). He is truly the *Saviour*, for he is the Lamb of God who takes upon himself the sin of the world (cf. Jn 1:29). With the shepherds, let us bow down before the Lamb, let us worship God's goodness made flesh, and let us allow tears of repentance to fill our eyes and cleanse our hearts. This is something we all need!

He alone, he alone can save us. Only God's mercy can free humanity from the many forms of evil, at times monstrous evil, which selfishness spawns in our midst. The grace of God can convert hearts and offer mankind a way out of humanly insoluble situations.

Where God is born, hope is born. He brings hope. Where God is born, peace is born. *And where peace is born, there is no longer room for hatred and for war.* Yet precisely where the incarnate Son of God came into the world, tensions and violence persist, and peace remains a gift to be implored and built. May Israelis and Palestinians resume direct dialogue and reach an agreement which will enable the two peoples to live together in harmony, ending a conflict which has long set them at odds, with grave repercussions for the entire region.

We pray to the Lord that the agreement reached in the United Nations may succeed in halting as quickly as possible the clash of arms in Syria and in remedying the extremely grave humanitarian situation of its suffering people. It is likewise urgent that the agreement on Libya be supported by all, so as to overcome the grave divisions and violence afflicting the country. May the attention of the international community be unanimously directed to ending the atrocities which in those countries, as well as in Iraq, Libya, Yemen and sub-Saharan Africa, even now reap numerous victims, cause immense suffering and do not even spare the historical and cultural patrimony of entire peoples. My thoughts also turn to those affected by brutal acts of terrorism, particularly the recent massacres which took place in Egyptian airspace, in Beirut, Paris, Bamako and Tunis.

To our brothers and sisters who in many parts of the world are being persecuted for their faith, may the Child Jesus grant consolation and strength. They are our martyrs of today.

We also pray for peace and concord among the peoples of the Democratic Republic of Congo, Burundi and South Sudan, that dialogue may

lead to a strengthened common commitment
to the building of civil societies animated by a
sincere spirit of reconciliation and of mutual
understanding.

May Christmas also bring true peace to Ukraine,
offer comfort to those suffering from the effects
of the conflict, and inspire willingness to carry out
the agreements made to restore concord in the
entire country.

May the joy of this day illumine the efforts of the
Colombian people so that, inspired by hope, they
may continue their commitment to working for
the desired peace.

*Where God is born, hope is born; and where hope is
born, persons regain their dignity.* Yet even today
great numbers of men and woman are deprived
of their human dignity and, like the child Jesus,
suffer cold, poverty, and rejection. May our
closeness today be felt by those who are most
vulnerable, especially child soldiers, women

who suffer violence, and the victims of human trafficking and the drug trade.

Nor may our encouragement be lacking to all those fleeing extreme poverty or war, travelling all too often in inhumane conditions and not infrequently at the risk of their lives. May God repay all those, both individuals and states, who generously work to provide assistance and welcome to the numerous migrants and refugees, helping them to build a dignified future for themselves and for their dear ones, and to be integrated in the societies which receive them.

On this festal day may the Lord grant renewed hope to all those who lack employment – and they are so many! May he sustain the commitment of those with public responsibilities in political and economic life, that they may work to pursue the common good and to protect the dignity of every human life.

Where God is born, mercy flourishes. Mercy is the

most precious gift which God gives us, especially during this Jubilee year in which we are called to discover that tender love of our heavenly Father for each of us. May the Lord enable prisoners in particular to experience his merciful love, which heals wounds and triumphs over evil.

Today, then, *let us* together *rejoice in the day of our salvation*. As we contemplate the Crib, let us gaze on the open arms of Jesus, which shows us the merciful embrace of God, as we hear the cries of the Child who whispers to us: 'for my brethren and companions' sake, I will say: Peace be within you' (Ps 121[122]:8).

Christmas greetings after the Urbi et Orbi *Message:*

To you, dear brothers and sisters all over the world who have come to this Square and to all those who join us by radio, television and other media, I offer my most cordial good wishes.

It is Christmas of the Holy Year of Mercy, and so I pray that all can welcome into their lives the mercy of God which Jesus Christ has bestowed on us, so that we in turn can show mercy to our brothers and sisters. In this way, we will make peace grow! Happy Christmas!

St Peter's Square, Friday, 25 December 2015

'Peace to Men and Women'

Dear brothers and sisters, happy Christmas!

Today the Church once more experiences the
wonder of the Blessed Virgin Mary, Saint
Joseph and the shepherds of Bethlehem, as they
contemplate the newborn Child laid in a manger:
Jesus, the Saviour.

On this day full of light, the prophetic
proclamation resounds:

'For to us a child is born,
To us a son is given.
And the government will be upon his shoulder;

and his name will be called
'Wonderful Counsellor, Mighty God,
Everlasting Father, Prince of Peace.' (Is 9:6)

The power of this Child, Son of God and Son
of Mary, is not the power of this world, based on
might and wealth; it is the power of love. It is
the power that created the heavens and the earth,
and gives life to all creation: to minerals, plants
and animals. It is the force that attracts man and
woman, and makes them one flesh, one single
existence. It is the power that gives new birth,
forgives sin, reconciles enemies, and transforms
evil into good. It is the power of God. This power
of love led Jesus Christ to strip himself of his glory
and become man; it led him to give his life on the
cross and to rise from the dead. It is the power
of service, which inaugurates in our world the
Kingdom of God, a kingdom of justice and peace.

For this reason, the birth of Jesus was
accompanied by the angels' song as they
proclaimed:

'Glory to God in the highest,
and on earth peace among men with whom he is
pleased!' (Lk 2:14)

Today this message goes out to the ends of the
earth to reach all peoples, especially those scarred
by war and harsh conflicts that seem stronger than
the yearning for peace.

Peace to men and women in the war-torn land of
Syria, where far too much blood has been spilled.
Particularly in Aleppo, the site of horrendous
fighting in recent weeks, it is most urgent that,
in respect for humanitarian law, assistance and
support be guaranteed to the sorely-tried civilian
population, who continue to live in desperate straits
and immense suffering and need. It is time for
weapons to be still forever, and the international
community to seek actively a negotiated solution, so
that civil coexistence can be restored in the country.

Peace to the women and men of the beloved Holy
Land, the land chosen and favoured by God.

May Israelis and Palestinians have the courage and determination to write a new page of history, where hate and revenge give way to the will to build together a future of mutual understanding and harmony. May Iraq, Libya and Yemen – whose peoples suffer war and the brutality of terrorism – be able once again to find unity and concord.

Peace to the men and women in various parts of Africa, especially in Nigeria, where fundamentalist terrorism exploits even children in order to perpetrate horror and death. Peace in South Sudan and the Democratic Republic of the Congo, so that divisions may be healed and all people of good will may strive to undertake the path of development and sharing, preferring the culture of dialogue to the mindset of conflict.

Peace to women and men who to this day suffer the consequences of the conflict in Eastern Ukraine, where there is urgent need for a common desire to bring relief to the civil population and to put into practice the commitments which have been assumed.

We implore harmony for the dear people of Colombia, which seeks to embark on a new and courageous path of dialogue and reconciliation. May such courage also motivate the beloved country of Venezuela to undertake the necessary steps to put an end to current tensions, and build together a future of hope for the whole population.

Peace to all who, in different areas, are enduring sufferings due to constant dangers and persistent injustice. May Myanmar consolidate its efforts to promote peaceful coexistence and, with the assistance of the international community, provide necessary protection and humanitarian assistance to all those so gravely and urgently in need of it. May the Korean peninsula see the tensions it is experiencing overcome in a renewed spirit of collaboration.

Peace to all who have been injured or have suffered the loss of a loved one due to the brutal acts of terrorism that have sown fear and death in the heart of many countries and cities. Peace – not merely the word, but real and concrete peace – to our abandoned and excluded brothers and sisters, to those who suffer hunger and to all the victims of violence. Peace to exiles, migrants and refugees, to all those who in our day are subject to human trafficking. Peace to the peoples who suffer because of the economic ambitions of a few, because of sheer greed and the idolatry of money, which leads to slavery. Peace to those affected by social and economic unrest, and to those who endure the consequences of earthquakes or other natural catastrophes.

And peace to the children, on this special day on which God became a child, above all those deprived of the joys of childhood because of hunger, wars or the selfishness of adults.

Peace on earth to men and women of goodwill, who work quietly and patiently each day, in their families and in society, to build a more humane and just world, sustained by the conviction that only with peace is there the possibility of a more prosperous future for all.

Dear brothers and sisters, 'For to us a child is born, to us a son is given': he is the 'Prince of Peace'. Let us welcome him!

⁂

Christmas greetings after the Urbi et Orbi *Message:*

To you, dear brothers and sisters, who have gathered in this Square from every part of the world, and to those in various countries who are linked to us by radio, television and other means of communication, I offer my greeting.

On this day of joy, we are all called to contemplate the Child Jesus, who gives hope once again to every person on the face of the earth. By his grace, let us with our voices and our actions give witness to solidarity and peace. Merry Christmas to all!

St Peter's Square, Sunday, 25 December 2016